Sea Otters

Sea Otters

Peter Murray

THE CHILD'S WORLD®, INC.

Published in the United States of America by The Child's World®, Inc.
PO Box 326
Chanhassen, MN 55317-0326
800-599-READ
www.childsworld.com

Product Manager Mary Berendes
Editor Katherine Stevenson
Designer Mary Berendes
Contributor Bob Temple

Photo Credits
ANIMALS ANIMALS © Johnny Johnson: 6, 26
ANIMALS ANIMALS © Ken Cole: 19, 29
© 2001 Brandon D. Cole: 2, 23
© Daniel J. Cox/naturalexposures.com: 10 (main photo), 13, 24
© G. C. Kelley, The National Audubon Society Collection/Photo Researchers: 10 (small photo)
© 2001 John Warden/Stone: 9
© 1996 Kevin Schafer: cover
© 1999 Kevin Schafer: 30
© 2001 Norbert Wu/www.norbertwu.com: 20
© Pat & Tom Leeson, The National Audubon Society Collection/Photo Researchers: 16
© 2001 Stuart Westmorland/Stone: 15

Library of Congress Cataloging-in-Publication Data
Murray, Peter, 1952 Sept. 29-
Sea otters / by Peter Murray.
p. cm.
Includes index.
ISBN 1-56766-892-5 (library bound : alk. paper)
1. Sea otter—Juvenile literature. [1. Sea otter. 2. Otters.]   I.Title.
QL737.C25 M87 2001
599.769'5—dc21
00-010775

On the cover...

Front cover: This adult sea otter is keeping its paws dry as it floats in Monterey Bay, California.
Page 2: This sea otter looks as though it's winking as it yawns after a nap.

Table of Contents

Just off the coast of Alaska, a small brown animal is floating on its back. A flat stone rests on its belly. The animal is holding a clam in its front paws. It lifts the clam, then slams it down on the rock. The animal looks at the clam to see if the shell has broken. After another try, the clam breaks open and the animal enjoys its dinner. What is this clever creature? It's a sea otter!

⇐ This sea otter from Alaska is getting ready to eat the clam it's holding.

What Are Sea Otters?

Sea otters are **mammals.** Mammals are animals that have hair or fur and feed their babies milk from their bodies. Mice, cows, monkeys, and people are mammals, too.

Sea otters are related to skunks, badgers, and weasels. They also have a very close relative—the river otter. But sea otters and river otters are different in many ways. For one thing, sea otters spend most of their lives floating in the salty ocean. River otters live mostly in freshwater rivers and can often can be found walking on the shore.

These two otters look as if they are ⇒
holding hands as they float along.

To many people, sea otters look a little like floating teddy bears. But they are much bigger—sea otters can grow to be about 100 pounds. Sea otters have round, furry faces with short noses, round eyes, and small round ears. They also have long whiskers that help them find food in the underwater darkness. They have **webbed feet,** too. Webbed feet have a thin piece of skin stretched between the toes. A sea otter's webbed feet act like swim fins to move the otter quickly through the water.

⇐ *Main photo:* This beautiful adult lives in Alaska.
Small photo: You can see this otter's webbed foot as it grooms itself.

Where Do Sea Otters Live?

Sea otters live along the coasts of the northern Pacific Ocean. Their favorite places are underwater forests of **kelp**, a giant seaweed. Kelp grows on the ocean bottom in water 50 to 100 feet deep. It grows all the way to the surface, where its leaves spread out in a greenish brown layer.

Kelp forests are home to many creatures sea otters like to eat. The otters dive deep into the kelp forest and use their eyes, nose, whiskers, and paws to find food. When it's time to eat, they simply take their meal to the surface and enjoy!

This sea otter has wrapped itself in kelp before taking its nap. ⇒

What Do Sea Otters Eat?

For sea otters, having plenty of food is important. An adult must eat 15 to 20 pounds of food a day! Fortunately, the kelp forests have all the food the otter needs. Clams, crabs, squid, snails, and abalone (AB-uh-loh-nee) are all favorite foods of sea otters.

One of an otter's favorite snacks is the sea urchin. Sea urchins are purple, spiny creatures that feed on kelp. By eating urchins, sea otters help the kelp beds stay healthy.

This otter has caught a small clam to eat. ⇒

Sea otters are one of the few animals to use tools. When an otter finds a shellfish attached to the sea floor, it uses a rock to knock it loose. Then it carries its dinner back to the surface. The otter floats on its back and turns its belly into a dinner table. It hammers the shell against the rock until it breaks open. When it has finished eating, the otter simply rolls over in the water to wash its belly.

⇐ This otter is using the rock on its belly to open the clam it is holding in its paws.

Do Sea Otters Live Alone?

Sea otters like to be with other sea otters. When you see one otter, you can be sure it's not alone. Sea otters spend most of their time in floating groups called **rafts.** A raft can include as many as 30 otters or as few as three. But sea otters don't live in groups to protect themselves. Scientists believe they live together so they have others to play with! Sea otters don't have dens or nests like other animals. Instead, they spend their lives on the ocean.

The otters in this small raft are sleeping in the late afternoon. ⇒

Sea otters are excellent swimmers. They move their large, webbed rear feet to push through the water. They use their broad tails to change directions as they speed through the kelp forest in search of food. Their swimming ability also helps them escape from killer whales, sharks, and other dangerous hunters, or **predators.**

How Do Sea Otters Stay Warm?

Other sea mammals such as seals and walruses have a thick layer of fat called **blubber.** Blubber keeps these mammals warm in the cold ocean and provides them with energy when food is scarce.

Sea otters don't have a layer of blubber, so they must rely on their heavy fur coats to keep them warm. Sea otters can have more than 650,000 hairs per square inch of their bodies. That's more hair than a person has on his or her entire body! An otter spends a lot of time grooming itself. Using its paws, mouth, and tongue, it squeezes water out of its fur and blows air into it. This thin layer of air keeps the otter warm.

This otter is grooming itself as it floats in a California kelp forest. ⇒

What Are Baby Sea Otters Like?

A female sea otter gives birth to a single baby, called a **pup.** The newborn weighs about four pounds and looks like a fuzzy ball. For the first few months, the pup spends almost all of its time on its mother's chest as she floats on the surface. Before the mother dives for food, she wraps her pup in some kelp or floating seaweed. The pup cries out as soon as its mother dives away. When the mother returns to the surface, she finds her baby by hearing its cries.

The young otter learns how to find food by watching its mother. By the time it is a year old, it can catch its own shellfish and open the hard shells with a rock.

⇐ Here a mother otter holds her baby as they rest on some kelp in Alaska.

Over 200 years ago, thousands of sea otters lived in the coastal waters of the northern Pacific. Unfortunately, during the 1800s, tens of thousands of sea otters were killed for their beautiful fur. Soon they were so rare that people could sell even a single animal's fur for a large amount of money. In 1911, several nations finally agreed to stop the hunting—but was it too late?

⇐ This sea otter has just come up from a dive in Alaskan waters.

For years, not a single sea otter could be found. But a few scattered groups had survived! In 1931, a raft of otters was spotted near Alaska. A few years later, another group was found off the California coast. The sea otters were back!

Today, nearly 2,000 sea otters live in the kelp beds off the California coast. Thousands more live off the coasts of Canada and Alaska.

This otter is getting ready to eat the piece of fish it's holding. ⇒

Sea otters still face many dangers. A single oil spill can kill thousands. Other types of pollution can destroy the kelp beds and poison the shellfish otters eat. Many otters are accidentally caught in fishing nets and drown. And some people illegally shoot sea otters because they think the otters eat too many clams and sea urchins. Will sea otters survive into the next century? They will if we protect them!

Glossary

blubber (BLUB-ber)
Blubber is a thick layer of fat found under the skin of most sea mammals. Sea otters lack blubber and must rely on their fur to keep them warm.

kelp (KELP)
Kelp is a giant seaweed that grows from the floor of the ocean all the way to the surface. "Forests" of kelp are home to a large number of sea creatures, including sea otters.

mammals (MAM-mullz)
Mammals are animals that have warm bodies, have hair or fur, and feed their babies milk from the mother's body. Otters are mammals, and so are people.

predators (PRED-eh-ters)
Predators are animals that hunt and eat other animals. Killer whales and sharks are predators that hunt sea otters.

pup (PUP)
A baby sea otter is called a pup. A sea otter pup often rests on its mother's chest as she floats in the water.

rafts (RAFTS)
A group of otters that live together is called a raft. The otters in a raft spend their time floating and swimming in the ocean.

webbed feet (WEBD FEET)
When an animal has webbed feet, its toes are connected together by a layer of skin. A sea otter's webbed feet help it to swim easily through the water.

Web Sites

http://www.seaworld.org/animal_bytes/sea_otterab.html

http://www.discovery.com/stories/nature/otters/otters.html

http://www.seaotters.org/

http://otternet.com/species/seaotter.htm